LIFE WITH DUTCH

Living with a grouchy Amazon parrot

LIFE WITH DUTCH

ISBN 979-8-9913993-9-5 paperback
Also available in e-book
Enola Publishing LLC

LIFE WITH DUTCH *is not a work of fiction. The characters in this book are real and have promised not to sue me.*

TABLE OF CONTENTS

DEDICATION:

This book is dedicated to anyone who adopts an animal, especially Linda, Michelle and Jake. We can learn a lot if we listen and try to understand.

LIFE WITH DUTCH

FORWORD

I'm a 76 year old woman who adopted a 20 year old Amazon parrot. I am approaching the end of my life but a 20 year old Amazon parrot is just beginning middle age. I guess I thought I'd have to decide who gets to care for the bird when I'm gone. But, as it turned out, the bird decided that one.

I am retired and living alone in an apartment and I got the bright idea of adopting a parrot. I guess you could say I was lonely and looking for trouble. I found it.

Dutch had been in the same home with his original owner, a man, for 20 years. When he died, the surviving relatives sent Dutch to a rescue. That should have told me something, and the name "Dutch" should have also told me something. It's an old fashioned slang word meaning "trouble."

I went to the rescue looking for an African Grey parrot. I owned a Grey and a Amazon when I was younger. Much younger. The Grey was intelligent, talkative and had a gentle nature. The Amazon was aggressive and loud. Maybe I didn't remember that.

Anyway, the rescue didn't have a Grey, but it had an Amazon for adoption; Dutch. I visited with Dutch for a month before adopting him, and he bit me, but only once. He didn't draw blood, and I shrugged it off. The old saying is "If you own a parrot, it's not a question of if you're gonna be bitten, but when."

The surviving relatives, who dropped Dutch off at the rescue, didn't leave a written history. The rescue told me he had been the property of a man for 20 years, preferred men, and was adopted by another man and returned to the rescue after 5 days. That should have told me something. But...

The rescue said the man who adopted him had 3 dogs and Dutch had become aggravated because of them and was returned. That made sense to me at the time, but I realized later that Dutch could make short work of three dogs.

In addition, there was no vet history for Dutch, no evidence that he knew how to speak and his wings were fully clipped.

I don't have any dogs or cats. I live in a small apartment by myself with quiet neighbors, and some have small dogs or cats. I asked my landlord if I could have a parrot and he said yes, so I adopted Dutch.

It wasn't long before I thought I would have been happier with a pit bull or a tarantula.

THE FIRST 30 DAYS

Day 1:

I adopted Dutch (translate: paid for him) and brought him home around 1 in the afternoon. I put him on the playstand by the balcony doors so he could see the birds and squirrels outside and watch the traffic. My friend Linda was with me. She was able to pick him up from the playstand without incident.

Later, when I tried to put him in the "sleep" cage in the next room, Dutch grew panicky, so I put him in the living room cage, uncovered, and we went to bed at 9 pm. We slept well.

Day 2:

We got up at 9:30 am. I put Dutch on the playstand until I had to leave for my regular appointment with the chiropractor. Dutch grew anxious and loud when I put him back in his cage so I covered him and he was quiet after that.

After the appointment and running a few errands, I got home around 5. Linda visited us and watched Dutch play on the playstand. At one point, he climbed up to the thin bar on the top of the stand that toys can be hung from and lost his balance. Linda was able to catch him on her hand and put him back on the playstand perch.

At 11 pm I asked Dutch to step up so I could put him back in his cage. He bit me, but he didn't break the skin and settled down once in the cage. I didn't know why he bit me, but I shrugged it off and went to bed.

Day 3:

I got up at 7 am and put Dutch on the playstand. I fed him there while I cleaned his cage and was relieved to see a sufficient number of poops at the bottom of it.

Dutch has been eating well and taking naps too. He bit me again without breaking the skin when I asked him to step up so I could handle him a little.

As I walked around with him on my hand, I tried to figure out why he bit me, Maybe he thought I was putting him away? But I couldn't find a reasonable answer, and just shrugged it off.

I put him on the playstand and did a couple of clicker training tricks with him and he took treats from my hand. Then I gave him piece of cardboard, a paper nail file and a small wooden spoon to destroy. He loved that.

I think Dutch is angry and confused. Imagine being taken from a busy rescue where you were surrounded by birds and people to a small apartment with only your kidnapper for company. You would be frustrated, angry, and sad too!

Day 4:
We got up at 7 am. I left Dutch in his cage while I made my coffee and his food. I put his food and water on the playstand and he allowed me to move him from the cage to the stand by the balcony without biting me.

Dutch grumbled and watched me as I went onto the balcony to feed the squirrels and birds outside. It was raining and the wind was blowing. Just a nasty day. Lots of traffic, but the squirrels and birds didn't come out for a few hours. I thought that was strange, but, as I said, it was a nasty day.

When I went too close to the playstand, Dutch jumped onto my arm and bit me. Once again, he didn't break the skin but I reacted by dropping my arm and he slid down my arm and latched onto my jeans and then onto the carpet. When he got to the carpet, he started hollering and seemed frightened.

I was afraid of getting bit again so I grabbed a vet wrapped stick and asked him to "step up." He did and I said, "Good bird!" in a silly, high-pitched voice. He looked at me like, "Really? I just bit you!"

I put Dutch back on the playstand and worked with the clicker and pointer stick on touch. I would say "touch" and show him the stick. If he touched the stick, I clicked. If he bit it, I did not. When he finally let me touch the top of his head with the stick, I clicked and said, "Good bird!" He seemed to like that. Sometimes he will accept a treat, sometimes not. But he always likes to hear my silly, high-pitched "Good bird!" praise.

Throughout the day, Dutch lunged at me to protect his playstand if I walked too close. He angrily chewed on his wood and paper toys, wooden spoons and pieces of cardboard, but he didn't care for popsicle sticks and just threw them down.

If I left the room, he would call, but not loudly. If I called back, he would get louder. But if I answered quietly, he was quieter too.

Dutch enjoys his mist-baths and eats his veggie mix like a champ. He gets a lot of exercise and seems to be getting stronger. He loves looking through the patio doors at the traffic and people below. He watches the wild birds at our feeders and only grunts a little when I leave the room.

Dutch took 2 naps during the day and went to bed at 9:30 pm. I did too!

Day 5:

Dutch had a peaceful night. His cage hasn't been covered at night and he can see when I get in bed, get up to go to the bathroom and when I wake up in the morning. He doesn't make any sounds at those times, except to maybe ruffle his feathers as if to say, "Hey, you woke me up!"

The first thing I do in the morning is turn all the plant lights on, make coffee and make his veggie mix with a sprinkle of seeds and a few pellets. I put his food and water on his playstand and move it to the balcony door so he can watch the squirrels, birds and traffic. Then I fill the bird feeders if they need filling and toss seed and nuts out to the squirrels. After that, I get Dutch and put him on the playstand.

Today, he didn't call for me whenever I got off the couch to get coffee or to eat or go to another room for something. He spent half his time facing inward to the apartment and half outward, watching out the balcony doors.

When I went by the playstand to latch the balcony door and bent over to put the security stick in place, Dutch climbed down on the playstand, lunged at me and tried to bite. He couldn't reach me and when I stood up, he climbed up to the top of his stand and started shredding his toys.

Then he climbed to the thin bar some of his toys are hung from and was losing his balance. I grabbed my vet-wrapped stick and put it near him. When he climbed on the stick and let me put him on the playstand perch, I said "Good bird!" That seemed to please him. Then I went back to the balcony door and bent down again. He just watched me. I stood up and said "Good bird!"

At 11:30, T put Dutch back in his cage because I

had a chiropractor appointment. He went in quietly and I said, "Good bird!" Dutch went to his feed bowl right away. He was uncovered when I left. I will ask my neighbors if he was noisy.

After I got home, my next door neighbor said she knocked on my door while I was gone and Dutch hollered something back at her, but he was quiet after that..

After I came home from my appointment, Linda, and my landlord and his wife visited, When I tried to put Dutch back in his cage, he had his first loud fit. He refused to go to his cage but I understood, I had taken him out and put him back in 4 times already, and he is used to going in and out once a day so when I tried to put him away AGAIN, he must have been frustrated and confused, but he finally went in the cage, and I cooked my dinner. (I didn't, at that point, feel confident enough to cook while he was out of his cage.)

After I ate dinner, I put Dutch on his playstand without incident. Whenever I went near the playstand, Dutch would climb to wherever I was and puff up and threaten to bite me. But when I said "touch" and touched him on the top of his head with the training stick, he held still and let me do it. After that, he seemed to calm down.

When I put him back in the cage for the night, he ate a big meal (after eating everything I gave him on the playstand) and went to sleep.

I did too. I was exhausted.

Day 6:

Dutch was quiet all morning. He just mumbled a little at times. We took a short nap around 10:30. After that, he ate well. That boy really loves his veggies!

Dutch took 4 naps today. I think yesterday tired him out. Today he watched the traffic and wild birds more than me and the room, which led me to believe he is feeling more relaxed and secure, but I was in for a surprise.

I worked with the clicker and pointer, but he wasn't interested. He just tried to ignore it.

I put Dutch in his cage and he bit me again, even though I used the step up stick. This time he drew blood. I covered the cage at 8 pm, but I didn't go to bed until midnight. Dutch was quiet. He was either sleeping or just planning how he many times he would bite me the next day.

Day 7:

After thinking about yesterday, I wondered if I was confusing Dutch when I tried to train him. Maybe I was putting too many things together in speech and gestures. So I took a few steps back and broke everything down to one gesture, one word to gave him time to focus. I can see him thinking when I work with him. Maybe I was moving too fast.

So today I made a list of simple words I wanted to work on with him and visualized consistent hand signals to go with them.

I also took a lot of toys off his playstand and rearranged some things in his cage. He was just pooping on most of them, but he really enjoys chewing up cardboard and wood blocks.

Day 8:

Dutch does a lot of grunting when I leave the room. It sounds like the sound a baby makes when it is unhappy and wants something. If I respond by talking to him, he usually grunts louder and sometimes it escalates to a yell. Sometimes Dutch makes a sound like a cat purring. I think he's happy when he does it.

Also, even though he gets a mist bath everyday, and grooms himself a lot, I've noticed a strong, bitter smell. Maybe it's the diet? He loves his vegetables. Or maybe it's hormones?

I haven't picked up Ditch on my hand since the last time he bit me. Each bite has gotten harder. The last time, he drew blood, so now I use a stick to transfer him and he sometimes he bites the stick. I always act very happy and say "Good bird!" when he steps up on the stick without biting it.

Today we had a very good training session. Once we bond, things will be fun for both of us. I need to be clear and consistent. Dutch is a good teacher. I just need to be a better student.

Day 9:

I think Dutch and I and I are making progress. He follows the pointer stick and touches it for a treat and he comes down on the playstand to see what I'm doing. Now I don't feel he's threatening me when he does it. Maybe he's just being curious.

Sometimes Dutch grinds his beak and I think that means he's content.

Dutch got real noisy when I went to the kitchen to make my dinner. I put him in his cage. When he was quiet, I took him out and put him on the playstand. But he got noisy again so I put him back in the cage and covered it. He stayed quiet even when he dumped his pellets. After I ate dinner, I brought him out and put him back on the playstand until it was time for bed. I gave him more pellets, but I don't think he likes them.

I didn't notice any odor today.

Day 10: (short updates)

Dutch and I had a peaceful day except when he got too loud twice and I had to put him in his cage and cover him.

He is eating well and is following the training stick consistently.

I give Dutch a mist bath everyday and he preens a lot. I think he's looking great.

Bedtime was 7:30 tonight. I had to cover him because he was fussing at me. After I covered him, I could hear him eating his veggies and even some of the pellets.

Day 11:

I caught Dutch masturbating on his playstand perch! I have been told that covering a cage will lead to hormonal behavior but I need to cover him sometimes. Maybe he will get over it when summer comes. Fortunately, after he ejaculated, he did not repeat that behavior today.

I put Dutch back in his cage while I worked in the kitchen, and he was quiet and did not call out even though I left him uncovered.

I finally picked up Dutch by hand today. He was very good and did not try to bite, just tried to climb up my arm, and I prevented that by lowering my elbow.

Dutch went to bed at 8:30 pm, covered.

Day 12:

Dutch came out to the playstand at 7:30, but he had to go back in his cage by 9 am since I had a chiropractor appointment. I left him uncovered. Then I sat outside the apartment on the stairs and listened. Dutch was loud so I went back in the apartment and covered him. He was quiet after that.

Dutch had a visit with Linda this afternoon and we had a quiet evening. I put him to bed at 8:30 and covered his cage so I could work on the computer.

Day 13 Friday: (yikes!)

Dutch was on the playstand at 8 am until 9:30 when I had to cage him for some work to be done in the apartment. After the handyman left, I took Dutch out and put him on the playstand. He got a mist shower (after two days without one) because I noticed the strong odor again. Is it odor hormonal or just normal? I don't know, but I'll give him a mist bath every day from now on. He likes it and his feathers are looking much better.

Dutch insisted on being held for a while today and that made me happy.

Day 14:

Dutch spends the morning on his playstand eating his breakfast and watching birds and squirrels.

Lately, he has been squawking a sound like "what up" or "Shar-wot" or maybe "Shut up!" when I'm out of the room. I don't like him to be loud, but that might be the name I was trying to teach him to call me. I also tried to teach him "Wyn-da" for Linda, but I think it's too hard for him.

I am happy to say he has been letting me handle him without trying to bite me or balance with his beak. I'm frustrated with and frightened of the biting, but the only thing that would make me give up on Dutch, at this point, is if my landlord threatens to evict me because of the noise he makes. Honestly, the yelling he does sounds like I'm having great sex, so I've been careful to let most of my neighbors know I have a parrot.

Today I had to cage and cover him twice because he was screaming, and it was only 11:30 in the morning. And if I made a sound, even though he's covered or a neighbor knocks at the door, he screamed again, even though he was covered.

I rolled Dutch's playstand into the art room because I wanted to finish my exercises there (it's the only space big enough to do some of them) and I was afraid he would scream if I left him in the living room. He seemed to like the movement of the stand rolling over the carpet and the tile floor and he spread his wings out a little and lowered his head to keep his balance on the moving stand.

When we got into the art room, I decided to take a few pictures of him and grabbed my phone. (I've only got 300 of him so far.) I clucked to get his attention and he clucked back to me! I was thrilled! We did that 3 times before he lost interest.

It's springtime and I've been coughing a lot and Dutch started trying to cough like me. I was almost worried about his health, but it wasn't a very good imitation and I recognized the cadence so, after I stopped reacting to him, he quit coughing. Later in the afternoon, he started sneezing, which I do a lot lately, and it was a pretty good sneeze!

Dutch is surprisingly easy to take care of and clean up after. And now that he's trying to make a connection to me, he's a real joy.

Day 15:

Today when I started eating breakfast, Dutch got loud. I thought he would be okay because he was on the playstand, he already had his breakfast and could see me in the kitchen. But he started calling loudly and wouldn't stop, so I put him in the cage. He still didn't stop, so I covered him. He was quiet then.

When I finished eating I uncovered him and said, "You're a good bird! Wanna come out?"

When I took him out, he bit me and when I put him on the playstand, he bit me again and wouldn't let go. I moved him around the stand until he finally let go of my finger and got on a perch.

He had pinched me really hard, but didn't draw blood. I think he was mad at me for putting him away and, after a while, he seemed to be hormonal again.

Later on, I said to him, "You bit me! Ouch!" and shook my hand. He cocked his head and stood a little taller, like he understood and was proud.

I think Amazons are outwardly emotional and Greys are inwardly emotional. Conures are happy little clowns and ringnecks are nerds. Macaws are awkward and simple giants, full of love. Cockatoos are stand up comedians, and most of them are gay. Cockatiels are the gossips of the neighborhood and budgies are playful neighborhood children.

But I digress...

Day 16:

When I took the garbage out today, I put Dutch in his cage, but did not cover him. Only five minutes later, I got back inside the building and the man who lives in the apartment below me was at my door. He looked down at me and said, "Are you in 208?"

"Yes...?"

"I ran upstairs because I thought someone in 208 was calling for help."

Then I realized that Dutch's loud vocalizations sounded like "Help! Help!"

I told him I was sorry and thanked him for the concern.

I guess I will have to cover Dutch every time I leave the apartment or face coming home to a bashed in door and police officers searching for the victim while Dutch watches them in silent fascination.

I took Dutch out of his cage and put him on his playstand. In spite of his distress and anger, Dutch didn't bite me then or when I picked him up and put him in his cage for the night at 8:30.

Then I sat down at my computer and typed a note to put on my door when I have to leave the apartment. It says, "My new parrot knows only one word: Help! If you have concerns, please call me" and added my cell phone number.

Day 17:

Dutch was very quiet this morning, even though workers were outside our door, sawing wood, grinding concrete and making a lot of noise. I think we have everything worked out. Things are good. I'm very happy to have Dutch in my life.

Day 18:

I had a chiropractor appointment today and quite a few errands to run, so Dutch was caged and covered until I got home at 5. I didn't get any phone calls about a parrot wanting help.

In the evening, we had visitors. Dutch was happy about that and went right to sleep when I put him away after they left.

Day 19:

Dutch was hormonal today. He masturbated all afternoon, but I never saw him finish.

Today I removed a few of his old toys and put some new ones in his cage. He looked at the new metal toys and chewed on them a little, but left them alone after discovering that he couldn't destroy them. He loves to chew up cardboard, wood and vet wrapped perches the most.

Dutch clucked with me today and coughed and

sneezed too. I think he wants to learn how to talk but it's harder for him since he is well past the age of easy learning. Everything is harder for him now that he is entering middle age. Just wait until you get to old age, Dutch!

Day 20:

Dutch was hormonal again today and had a very distinct smell again. Not a loud smell, but it was obvious when you got close to him.

He was busy all day shredding his wood blocks, cardboard and vet wrapped perches.

Day 21:

Although today was another day of hormones and shredding, I was able leave the apartment for a few minutes without having to cage and cover Dutch. When I had to leave for a longer time to do the laundry, I caged him, but did not cover him. I tested him by standing outside the door and listening for a few minutes. He didn't start yelling but I taped the sign on my door just in case he did.

I put Dutch on his playstand after I came back from doing laundry. Two hours later, I caged him again and installed a vet wrapped swing on his playstand. After that, I grabbed a vet wrapped stick to transfer him, but he wouldn't "step up" on it. Instead, he tried to shred it. So I left him in his cage.

I tried 4 more times in the next 2 hours, but he refused to "step up". On the 5th try, he stepped up and I said, "Oh, what a good bird!" Then he said, "Aw ,aw aw," in his happy bird voice, stepped off the stick and began to shred his new swing.

Dutch was angry the rest of the afternoon and evening, shredding his perches and climbing down the playstand to balance in the thin edge of the skirt. At one point, he lost his balance and fell off it onto the carpet. It didn't seem to hurt him and he allowed me to pick him up (with the stick) and place him back on the playstand.

Today, every time I got off the couch, which is right next to the playstand, (but a safe distance away from it!), Dutch would stop what he was destroying and look at me. It was as if he was saying, "Stay put. Don't you get it?" But I didn't get it. I had things to do. I only knew I wanted to get it, and if I couldn't get it, I would try some other way to understand him. Dutch has a lot of adjusting to do. I will watch and wait and maybe someday I will get what he is trying to tell me. And maybe he will get what I am trying to tell him?

Day 22:

Dutch has been angry all day, especially after I caged and covered him and left the apartment to go for a bike ride.

When I came home, I took him out, but had to put

him back in the cage so I could cook dinner. After I ate dinner I tried to take him out but he refused to step up 6 times and just bit the stick. I gave Dutch 10 minutes between each request to step up and when I asked him to step up the 7th time, he bit the stick and tried to pull it into the cage. I pushed the stick against him and almost forced him to step up. When I put him on the playstand, he attacked the vet wrap on his perches.

But, on the other hand, he was loud only once today, so that's progress. I don't think it will last...

Day 23:

Dutch has decided to go all the places he's not supposed to go: the thin rod that I hang toys from and the rim of the seed catcher on the playstand. He often loses his balance on both, so I took the thin rod down but I didn't know what to do about the seed catcher. Eventually, I found a perch the same length as one side of the seed catcher so I vet wrapped it and taped it to the seed catcher skirt. Dutch watched me attach the new perch from the highest perch on the playstand, but wouldn't go near the perch on the seed catcher.

It more than a week before he finally went down to the perch on the seed catcher skirt and used it.

Day 24:

Today when I left the room, Dutch made baby

grunts, then called quietly at first, but got louder and louder. I didn't respond because I figured he was just looking for a response, and it worked. Dutch gave up calling after a few minutes and stayed quiet until I returned to the room.

I wish I could do the same thing when he bites me, but my response is a reflex action to pain. I doubt that I can change my response and stand the pain.

Dutch surprised me later in the day by lifting his foot, asking to step up. I let him get on my hand and he didn't try to bite me. I said "Good bird!" I always use the same silly high-pitched voice and say "Good bird!" when he steps up without trying to bite. He gets excited and makes silly sounds with me at those times. It's fun to connect with him.

Day 25:
Today I had a chiropractor appointment and had to leave Dutch caged and covered for a long time. I went to lunch with Linda, ran some errands and took a bike ride in the afternoon, so Dutch was in the cage for a long time.

After I got home he grunted and called loudly when I went into another room, but I think I made it all up to him when I brought out the boiled peanuts he loves!

Day 26:
Dutch has been angrily shredding his vet wrapped

perches so much that I made a subscribe and save order for them. Shredding vet wrap keeps him busy and the perches are easy to wrap again in bright colors after he destroys them.

I'm still using the stick to pick him up and move him to and from the cage. Sometimes he bites it and tries to pull it away from me, so I just leave him in the cage at those times.

Today, he surprised me by lifting his foot beyond the stick to my hand, so I picked him up. He was very good and I did the silly "Oh, you're a good bird!" voice. Dutch joined right in with his happy voice.

It's obvious who's the boss in this relationship...

Day 27:

Today, once again, Dutch indicated with his foot that he wanted to step up onto my hand instead of the stick. In fact, he was so quick about it that, before I knew it, he was on my hand. I did the silly owner voice, "What a good bird!" and he joined right in with a few loud noises of his own.

Sometimes Dutch purrs like a cat, sometimes he grunts like a baby who wants something, but today I heard him growl at something outside. He was clearly not pleased!

When Dutch does his mating posture, he gets loud. I've started bumping his playstand when he does that, and he quits after 3 or 4 bumps.

Dutch hasn't spoken, clucked, coughed or sneezed

in a few days. I miss it.

Day 28:

Dutch is sleeping a lot during the day even though I put him in his cage and cover it every night between 8 and 9. The room is dark and quiet so I know he is getting the recommended 12 hours of sleep. It makes me wonder how old he really is.

Dutch has a closed band on his leg and it has the numbers 4 02. I'm wondering if that means he is 23 years old. I've read that a closed band means a bird was domestically bred. I'm beginning to wonder about that. I've read and seen videos of Amazons living wild in Florida and even Germany so, in my over-active imagination, I can picture Dutch being captured from the wild in Florida and banded and sold as a domestically bred parrot. That would explain a lot...

Day 29:

Linda's husband cut a bunch of wood into blocks and drilled holes in them for Dutch. I string them on twine and hang them on his playstand for him to chew up. He no longer threatens me when I place them on his play stand and he destroys 2-3 every day, so I know he likes them!

Day 30:

Dutch was very angry today and got loud each

time I left the room, even though he could hear me doing things. If he couldn't see me, he got loud. I hope I don't have to cage and cover him every time I need to do something in of another room. I don't want to move him to the cage and cover him or roll his playstand into the other room every time I need to make a quick trip for something. Then it wouldn't be a quick trip!

THE SECOND 30 DAYS

Day 31:

Dutch came out of his cage at 7:30 this morning and ate breakfast on his playstand. He took naps all morning until I ate my lunch yogurt. I always give him a nut when I eat my yogurt (while sitting on the couch next to the playstand.)

Later, I brought out the boiled peanuts (one of his favorite treats) and said. "Want some?"

I'm trying to teach Dutch specific words like: "Wanna come out?" "Step up." "Good bird!" "Hi!" "Want some?" and "Wanna go for a ride?" Today, I swear he said, "Shar-wot" while he was caged and covered, but I couldn't get him to repeat it.

Oh well, patience is a virtue. I'm learning to read his body language and keep things simple. Yep, he's training me!

When he started sneezing and coughing more frequently, I realized I was sneezing and coughing more too. I am afraid I'm becoming allergic to him.

I had to leave the apartment, so I put Dutch in his cage. He was being good, so I didn't cover him. Big mistake. He started hollering and he was really loud. I had to rush back inside and cover him. "Great,"

I thought. "Now he will think he's being punished every time he goes to his cage. No wonder he never speaks to me!"

Dutch grumbled, but didn't holler anymore. But he didn't want to come out of his cage after that. I asked him three times, "Wanna come out?" It was a definite "no" with him biting the stick in anger. Good thing I hadn't offered my hand! About an hour later, Dutch decided to come out peacefully (on the stick) and we spent another hour on the stand and the couch.

Finally, I put him in his cage for the night. Then I went into the kitchen to wash dishes. I didn't cover him and he started hollering again. I decided to let it run it's course, if I could stand it. All of a sudden, I heard Dutch say "Damn!"

I couldn't believe it! I went into the living room and stared at him. He clucked at me! I gasped and stared at him. Who is this bird? I was pleased that he was talking, but I didn't really appreciate the word.

So I stood there, dripping dish water, and Dutch whistled at me! I can't whistle, but I said, "Damn!"

Then Dutch clucked at me. I clucked back. He was training me again, but I didn't care. Dutch was communicating with me! Finally.

I stood there and tried every word I wanted him to learn, but Dutch just looked at me like I was the dumbest student he ever had. Finally, I gave up and went to get him a cashew, one of his favorite nuts.

"Hi!" I said. No response. "Whatcha doin?" No response. "Wanna nut?" No response, but a lot of eye pinning. (Humans are stupid.)

I backed away and waited. He puffed up his feathers started hissing at me. Well, that was new. I had no idea what it meant. So I tried again, "Hi!" No response. "Whatcha doin?" No response. "Wanna nut?" Dutch hissed some more. I hissed back. His eyes got big. I could almost see him thinking that maybe he could teach this human something after all.

I raised my hand. "Hi!" No response. I did that about fifty times and Dutch just watched me in fascination until he got bored. He lifted his foot to move away, and I said "Hi!" and thrust the nut at him. Thank goodness he took it. I was exhausted.

I don't know if he connected the foot lifting to "Hi!" I was hoping he did but, honestly, I think Dutch was training me again and not the other way around.

Day 32:
Linda and I took Dutch to get his nails done and his beak checked today. We took him in Linda's car in his new bird carrier and buckled him into the back seat. I wonder if he thought we were returning him to the rescue?

After getting Dutch's nails done we went to eat

at a Mexican restaurant. Dutch had to come inside with us because it was 80 and humid outside. We got a booth and he was quiet in the carrier but refused both water and a chip.

When we got home, Dutch slept all afternoon - until I brought out the boiled peanuts!

Day 33:

Dutch and I were both tired all day long. We took naps throughout the day. When I went into another room, Dutch would be quiet for a few minutes, then he would start with baby grunts. The baby grunts would escalate to quiet calls for "help" and the calls for "help" would escalate in volume to panic decibels. I cringed and hoped my neighbors weren't home.

I know that parrots in the wild are constantly communicating. Eventually, I decided to talk to Dutch in a quiet voice. I knew that answering his call was a reward, but it was the reaction he wanted. To my surprise, he would be quiet for a while after he answered me in a quieter voice. It worked! Maybe I was trainable, after all.

I had to do laundry, so I put Dutch in the cage and covered him, hoping he wouldn't start hollering for me. The laundry room is downstairs in our building and I had to go down and back up to the apartment 6 times. I let him know I would "Be back soon"and greeted him with "Hi" each time I came back, always speaking to the covered cage. Dutch was quiet. He even refused to come out of the cage when I came back. But I was able to stroke his beak and forehead when he pressed against the cage bars.

Finally, around 7:30, I got Dutch to "step up" and come out to the playstand. When I put him away for the night, he grunted and grumbled until 10 pm.

Day 34:

This morning, whenever I went into another room, Dutch would call for me but, once again, answering him quietly got him to call to me in a quieter voice and, in the afternoon, he didn't call when I went into another room.

More small break throughs came when I got him to climb to the top of the playstand for a treat and, later, I was able to touch his forehead with my finger.

Day 35:

Dutch was hormonal again today. He spent a lot of time crouching, fluttering and muttering on the top of his playstand. He took a few naps and called loudly if I left the room. Sigh.

Day 36:

Today I put Dutch in his cage whenever I had to leave the room. I had to cover him too, or he would holler for me.

If I went close to his cage, Dutch would lunge out and bite the cage bars. I reacted with a sharp "No!" until I finally said, "What's wrong with you? I would never hurt you!" He seemed to listen, so right then I tried to touch the top of his head. He let me do it, so I did it twice. He was quiet the rest of the day.

Day 37:

Today was peaceful. Dutch didn't get loud when I left the room. Once, when I had to leave for a longer time than usual, I caged and covered him. When I decided to cook and eat my dinner, I caged and covered him then too because that's a time when he usually gets loud.

I started giving Dutch a soaking bath today instead of just spraying him lightly. He really enjoyed it and purred and flapped his wings. I was even able to get a good photo of his wings stretched out. I feared that Dutch had been "pined" (that's when a vet surgically removes the ends of a bird's wings to prevent them from flying) but, from the photo, I could see that he had instead been clipped fully - all his flight feathers were gone.

I want to let Dutch grow out all of his flight feathers. I doubt that he will ever fly, after 20+ years of not flying, but it will help him glide if he ever falls and I might be able to get him to exercise his wings more by encouraging him to flap. That might improve his attitude and self-confidence because he seems to be afraid of falling. Maybe that's why he grabs the step up stick with his beak.

Day 38:

I'm retired and basically a loner, so Dutch and I spend most days in the living room by the balcony door. My desk is also in the living room as well as most of my exercise equipment and his cage. So we spend a lot of time together.

If the weather is comfortable, I like to ride my bike in the afternoon. It's springtime now, and I want to order a smaller carry cage that will fit on the back of the bike so he can ride with me. I've even ordered a custom license plate for Dutch! The carry cage I'm looking at has straps so it can be used as a backpack, so maybe I'll take him out on hikes.

Day 39:

I conducted an experiment today. I left Dutch on the playstand and went into another room. It wasn't long before he started hollering. He got very loud and it went on for quite a while. Finally, when he had been silent for 10 seconds, I walked through the living room and into the kitchen.

Dutch started a low grumble because he couldn't see me. But I had things to do and didn't want to cage and cover him again. So, when he paused in his grumble, I started making kitchen noises. And I started clucking and making kiss noises. He was quiet. If I made little noises, he was quiet! Erika! I'm getting trained!

Day 40:

Dutch ate 3 chunks of baked ham!

He also offered me his foot twice today and I quickly raised my hand and said "Hi!" each time. He's a master at training me!

Day 41:

Dutch was quiet today each time I went into other rooms, but he hollered a lot after I caged and covered him when I went downstairs to do laundry. Sigh.

He really enjoyed his shower today and fluffed up his feathers, lifted his wings and chortled while getting wet. That was fun.

Day 42:

Dutch was quiet and patient until the afternoon. I went into another room and he got really loud so I returned and caged and covered him. 30 minutes later he was still quiet so I uncovered him and invited him to come out, but he refused. He makes it very clear to me when he doesn't want to come out by biting the stick instead of stepping up. So I left him in the cage uncovered. After about an hour,

I knew that he wanted out when he started baby grunts and sat on his perch by the cage door.

We spent another two hours together, then Dutch got restless and seemed to want to go back "home" to his cage. I put him away, covered him and said good night.

Day 43:

Today Dutch was quiet whenever I went into another room, and I thought, "Hey, we are making progress!" However, I caged him but did not cover him when I went outside to take the garbage out. I had planned to go for a bike ride but Dutch was hollering when I got back inside the building from taking the garbage out. I had to go back upstairs and cover the cage. Then he was quiet.

The surprise came when I got back from my ride and uncovered him. Dutch said, "Hey" loud and clear!

After that, I got him to cluck at me, but nothing else. So now I know Dutch can say 3 words: "Help!" "Damn!" and "Hey!"

Day 44:

It was a peaceful day today. Dutch was quiet whenever I went into another room and he was quiet when I went for a bike ride, but, of course, he was caged and covered.

Dutch loves to chew up and destroy things. His favorite toy right now is a cylinder of compressed cardboard which he strips apart layer by layer. He goes through at least a half dozen of them a day and looks at the bottom of his playstand where they lie in shreds as if to say, "All done. What a nice mess!"

His second favorite toy is vet wrap. I wrap his perches with layers of vet wrap to give him a secure hold and he spends a large portion of the day shredding the vet wrap and tearing it off the perches.

Needless to say, I have a subscribe and save order for the cardboard cylinder toys and vet wrap!

Day 45:

Dutch was a good, quiet bird all day. The only surprise was when I had my dinner, he indicated a desire to eat some of my cheeseburger by making baby grunts. I gave him a chunk of my burger and I think he actually liked it!

Day 46:

Dutch was hollering so much in his covered cage today when I had to work in another room that I actually considered thumping it to get him to shut up. But I knew that might scare him and turn his safe place into something scary and unpredictable. His insecurity is probably causing his hollering in the first place. So that would be a dumb thing to do.

I just kept quiet and although it took a while, eventually the hollering stopped.

Day 47:

Dutch got hormonal after ate breakfast even though he had more than 12 hours of sleep. But he was quiet and a good boy after he got that out of his system!

Day 48:

Dutch was hormonal again after breakfast. Food comes first, I guess!

I put a small cardboard box in the bottom of his cage and he thoroughly enjoyed pushing it around and tearing it up while I took the garbage out and got my mail. But I covered the cage anyway. He seems to feel safer if it's covered. I cover the cage anytime I leave the apartment now, or he will holler.

Day 49:

Dutch masturbated after breakfast again today. It's always accompanied by baby grunts.

We had a quiet day. Dutch didn't scream when I went into other rooms. I had rolled his playstand into the other rooms a few times and he heard the sounds I make there, so I think he understands where I am and that I will return to the living room eventually.

Day 50:

Last night we had the loudest, most lightening filled thunderstorm I have ever heard or witnessed.

It lasted for at least an hour, maybe more. Dutch slept through it all!

Day 51:

Today Dutch had a screaming fit when I went into the bathroom to wash my face, brush my teeth and change clothes. I let him scream until he stopped. It took a while. Then I walked back into the living room and gave him a nut.

After that, I decided it's time for me to start expecting more from Dutch. But handling him would have consequences. I would have to risk getting bit. Did I want to do that after handling him for a month with a stick? No, I'm a big chicken. I will have to figure out how to have meaningful interactions with Dutch using the stick.

I wanted to clean his playstand and vacuum so I put Dutch in his cage early this evening. After vacuuming, I offered the stick to let him come out again. He attacked it. He does that on a regular basis whenever he is feeling cranky, but this time the stick fought back.

When Dutch grabbed the stick with his foot and bit it, the stick played tug-of-war with him. Dutch is very strong, but the stick eventually won. When it won and Dutch let go, the stick rapped 3 times on his perch. Then the stick stopped and rested on his perch.

Dutch grabbed the stick with his foot and started

biting it. Another tug-of-war. The stick won again. And rapped 3 times on his perch. Round 3 ensued. The stick won this round too. And rapped 3 times on his perch. Dutch must have been tired because he just looked at the stick. The stick withdrew.

Later I went to the cage to check on him. Dutch likes to put his beak through the bars. I usually stroke it and try to ruffle the feathers on his head until he tries to bite my finger. Sometimes he likes to hiss at me. I hiss back.

Today I rubbed his beak and kind of pulled on it. He seemed not to hate it and when I ruffled the feathers on his head, he hissed at me, but did not try to bite. I hissed and rubbed his head a couple more times. After that, I clucked at him and he clucked back! I was delighted. Anytime Dutch clucks or hisses back at me (it's not often), I'm over the moon!

I often wonder if he ever really learned to talk. He says Help, Hey and Damn, but can he talk? Can he learn to talk? Or is he past that learning stage? Is the hissing his attempt to say Hi?

After a while, I grabbed the stick again and asked Dutch to step up. He didn't attack it and stepped right up. I did the silly "Good bird!" voice he loves to hear and walked around for a few minutes, then put him back in his cage.

After that, I went to work at the computer and Dutch fell asleep. He was probably exhausted after going 3 rounds with the stick.

Day 52:

This morning Dutch stepped up onto the stick to leave his cage, but he bit the stick viciously after stepping down onto the playstand, so I placed the stick beside him again for another step up and he stepped up and off again without biting it. I said "Good bird! and we were both happy.

Day 53:

Dutch was hormonal and aggressive this morning. He came out of the cage quietly and went back in it quietly a couple of hours later, but something happened in his mind and he became aggressive when I asked him to come out an hour later. He attacked the stick fiercely and was so aggressive that I decided to leave the stick in the cage with him so he could either teach it a lesson or kill it. He attacked the stick and chewed on it at the bottom of his cage for a few minutes, then lost interest and went to his feed bowl.

I retrieved the stick and asked him to step up an hour later, but he bit the stick and started fighting with it again. After a few more attempts, I managed to get him to step up, but he still bit the stick before doing it. I put him on the playstand and then asked him to step up. He bit the stick again, but stepped up. I put him back on the playstand, then asked him to step up again. He didn't bite the stick and stepped up. I chortled "Good bird!" and he puffed up his feathers and chortled with me. I repeated the process several times with good results.

Later in the day, I put Dutch back in his cage and had to cover him because he started hollering again when he couldn't see me. I thumped on his cage and he growled, but shut up for a few minutes. Then he started hollering again so I thumped on the cage again. He growled at me but stayed quiet after that.

I decided to repeat the whole process a couple more times. I took Dutch out of his cage and, after an hour, put him away and covered him. He started hollering. After a while, I uncovered him and asked him to step up. He bit the stick, but stepped up. I put him on the playstand, then asked him to step up again. He bit the stick, but stepped up so I put him down again and then asked him to step up. He didn't bite the stick and stepped up. I said "Good bird!" in my silly voice and he puffed up and chortled with me. I repeated the process several times, and again, with good results.

I really don't know what to do with Dutch at this point. He's not a good pet and he's a lot of work. He's shedding profusely and, even though he gets a soaker shower once a day, he has a strong smell. I know it's hormonal, but I'm beginning to think I'm allergic to him.

I've had Dutch for almost 2 months. So I bought

another air cleaner, and this one has a filter made for pet allergies. Now I have 3 air cleaners but I still cough and sneeze more than before. My nose runs and lately, I've been getting head-achy and not sleeping well.

I don't want to give up on Dutch, but maybe someone else can do a better job with him and maybe my allergies would clear up if I did. But then I look at him, even when he isn't being good and his eyes are pinning at me with hatred and I think, "I really want to communicate with this beast."

I try so hard to connect with him but only get aggression or grunts. I cluck and half the time he just stars at me like "You're an idiot." He says only "Help", "Damn" and "Hey" when he wants attention.

Dutch is a mystery. I remind myself that, just as there are unreachable people, there are animals that are unreachable too.

In my opinion, birds and cats are basically wild animals, whether domestically bred or not. Birds can fly away from us and live quite successfully in the wild. Cats may not do quite as well in the wild, depending upon where they live, but, in our houses, they make their own rules, jumping on countertops, climbing up curtain and scratching up furniture as well as pooping and peeing in forbidden places. Unlike dogs, who have been our faithful companions and protectors for thousands of years, birds and cats do quite well in the wild without us. They live shorter lives, but they are free. And wild. It's just hard to accept.

I think Dutch is worth the effort. He just needs to throw me anther bone.

Day 54:

When Dutch is in his cage and I try to get him to talk to me, he mostly hisses at me by opening his mouth and raising his tongue. When he pushes air through, it creates a hissing sound. Sometimes his eyes pin and sometimes they remain large. Maybe he's trying to say hi?

When Dutch is on his playstand and he's happy, he will purr. If I try to communicate with him, he will purr in response. It doesn't matter if I talk or just move my hand. He will purr. Well, that's something. He's responding to me. It gives me hope.

I'm going to just try to get any response from Dutch when I try to communicate with him. When I ask him to move over on his perch or come up or down or lift a foot, he will get a response from me like "Good bird!" or a treat.

Today I asked him to move over and, after that, to let me scratch his head. He lunged at me and tried to bite. I said, "No! You can't do that!" and shook my finger at him. Maybe he thought that was a reward. Sigh. I have to learn to just walk away.

Later in the day, I asked to scratch his head. I indicate that by holding my hand above his head, curling and uncurling my index finger and saying, "Touch.". He usually raises his head and watches my finger. Today he let me scratch his head 3 times and even lowered his head and opened his neck feathers. I stopped after 3 times. I figured things could go south at any point. No need to push it.

Later, I put Dutch back in his cage so I could do my exercises in the other room. After that, I thought he would want to come out at noon and get back on the playstand, but he attacked the stick. I left it in his cage and he continued to attack it for quite a while, even picking it up and dropping it and running at it and attacking it. Is he mad at it because I don't offer my hand?

The young woman who handled him at the rescue always offered her arm. Her hand was pretty scared up. Probably form years of getting bit. My old arthritic hands don't need that. I considered offering my arm like she does, but no. I rejected that idea for now. Maybe in the future.

Day 55:
It was a busy day for me. Dutch got out for a couple of hours in the morning but I had another chiropractor appointment and errands to run, so Dutch had to stay caged and covered until around 2 pm.

When I got home, I put Dutch on the playstand

and went into the kitchen to make a pot of coffee.

Linda was visiting and watched Dutch while I was in the kitchen. She tried to pick him up, but he bit her. He didn't draw blood, but he pinched her hard, and I'm sure it hurt. Sigh. Like someone said: " It's not a question of if you'll get bit, but when."

Dutch was relatively quiet the rest of the day. When I went to put him back in his cage for the night, he whistled at me! Three times. I can't whistle, but I was delighted and tried. He just looked at me like I was an idiot.

After that, I spent an hour, searching Amazon for just the right whistle. Who is training who?

Day 56:

Today I decided that Dutch needs to step up without biting or grabbing the stick. It seems like it has gotten to be a habit. Maybe he is afraid of falling, but now I'm beginning to think it's just a habit.

So today when I asked him to step up on the stick and he grabbed it, I said "no" in a calm voice and took the stick away. The third and forth time that happened, Dutch got angry and tried to keep the stick by really biting down hard on it. I said "no" and grabbed my pointer training stick to get him to keep his head up while stepping up. That worked. The next time he stepped up, he did it without biting the stick. I said "Good bird!" in my silly voice and he chortled with me in celebration of his good behavior.

When we got to the playstand, I asked Dutch to step up again twice more, using the pointer stick to keep his head up. He did it, so maybe someday he will step up on a hand or arm without biting it first.

Day 57:

Today was a very good day for Dutch. He bit the stick only once when I asked him to step up this morning. He seems to understand that the pointer stick means he should keep his head up and just use his feet when stepping up. We had 3 sessions today, working on that. He really likes it when he does it right and I use the silly voice to say "Good bird! You're such a good boy! "

Day 58:

Dutch came out of his cage this morning without biting the stick! Yay!!! And he was good all day! He didn't call when I went into other rooms.

Sometime in the afternoon he seemed restless so I put him in his cage and he was happy there. When I tried to take him out again, he went to the bottom of his cage. That always means he doesn't want to come out. When he wants to come out, he will go to the highest perch in his cage or go to the perch by the cage door.

At one point he made a whistling sound, and did that 3 times. I was delighted. Of course, he got a "Good bird!"

Around 6 in the afternoon, Dutch wanted to come out of his cage. He was happy on the playstand until it was almost dark.

Dutch has indicated his desire to step up on my hand several times by lifting his foot when I talk to him, but I'm trying to turn that into a "Hi" trick. I don't trust him not to bite me yet.

Day 59:

Dutch was happy and cooperative all day. Around 4 in the afternoon he was restless and seemed to want to go to his cage. I put him there after he stepped up without biting the stick.

I left him uncovered in the cage when I took the garbage out. By the time I got to the stairs, I could hear him hollering. I waited outside the door until he was quiet and then went in. I said, "Hi' Hello!" and pretended he had been good all along.

Day 60:

Dutch is still trying to grab the stick with his mouth before he steps up. I tell him "No!" and ask him to do it again. He usually gets it right the 2nd time and I praise him with the silly voice and he joins in and chortles with me.

Today Dutch wanted to spend the middle part of

the day back in his cage. He came out again around 6 and stayed out until 8:30. I'm glad Dutch likes his cage and doesn't think going there is a punishment.

THE THIRD 30 DAYS

Day 61:

Today when I asked Dutch to step up on the stick, he bit it, so I put him on his open door and asked him to step up on the stick from there. He did it right without me having to use the pointer stick. I praised him, Good bird!" and he chortled loudly with me. Celebrating his accomplishments is the only time I don't mind if he gets loud.

Day 62:

Dutch had a quiet day. He stepped up perfectly coming out of his cage in the morning, was quiet all day, and spent a couple of hours in his cage in the afternoon. He came out later and stayed out until dark, showing me his desire to go back to his cage by getting restless on the playstand and making baby grunts. When I put him back in his cage for the night, he purred. I think we are developing a language. Yep, he's teaching me.

Day 63:

Once again, Dutch bit the step-up stick and had to be put on his cage door and be asked to step up properly from there. And again, he did it right the second time and we got silly, celebrating his success.

However, when he wanted to go back inside his cage around noontime, he stepped onto the stick and rapidly stepped over it and stood on my hand. I almost panicked, but he didn't bite me so I said, quietly, "I really don't want you on my hand," but I left him there and put him in his cage and told him "Good bird!" in the silly voice.

Later, I asked him, "Wanna come out?" but he wasn't ready. When he doesn't want to come out, he will go to the highest perch in his cage and turn his back on me or he will go to the bottom of his cage and hide his head in the back corner. If he's mad at me, he will bite the bars of his cage.

Later, when he was ready to come out, he bit the stick again so I pulled it away and said, "Now, do it right," and he did. When I put him on the playstand, he bit the stick again, so I made him step up and off it properly. Then I said, "Good bird!"

Later in the day, Dutch started getting loud. I was in the other room. I knew he could hear me, but he kept it up, getting louder every time I made a sound.

When I walked back into the room, he shut up, and when I sat down on the couch (where he wants me to stay all day) he whistled. It was one whistle, one note. I whistled back three times, but he would not repeat it. Even so, it felt like a special moment.

Once again, Dutch had thrown me a bone for being a good girl.

Day 64:

Today I took the vet wrap off the step-up stick, thinking that maybe Dutch bites it because he loves to tear up vet wrap. But he bit the stick anyway, so the vet wrap went back on.

Dutch is gaining a lot of weight. I don't know what the ideal weight for a 20 year old Amazon is, but I've decided to not worry about it until he has grown all new flight feathers.

I'm excited to see Dutch fully flighted. He will look magnificent. I don't think he will start flying (and attack me?) because I don't think he was ever allowed to fly. (Can you imagine standing on your legs to do everything for 20 years?) I just want him to be able to glide in case he falls. If he starts flying, well, I'll see how his behavior changes and address that issue when the time comes.

Dutch was good all day. He would call sometimes when I went into another room, but not loudly and not for long. And he wasn't hormonal. It was a good day.

Day 65:

Another peaceful, happy day! Dutch even let me scratch him on the top of his head and stroke his neck!

Day 66:

Another good day. Dutch let me scratch his bead and neck, briefly, with 2 fingers. Maybe he has trust issues. Who knows? He's more than 20 years old with an unknown history.

I put Dutch in his carrier this afternoon and we sat outside in front of the apartment building with the neighbors. They were very curious about Dutch and focused on him the whole time we were there. I told them about his bad habits: yelling, biting, shredding things and acting hormonal. At one point he tried to leave the carrier when I unzipped it to show everyone his pretty colors. That was when he tried to step up on one of the neighbor's hand. I quickly closed the carrier and said, "Be careful. He bites."

One of my neighbors suggested wearing gloves when handling Dutch and I'm considering it. He isn't trying to bite me right now, but I know the day will come when he does.

Day 67:

Amazons don't pluck their feathers like Greys and Cockatoos. I think that's because Amazon display their aggression outwardly, whereas Greys and Cockatoos are more sensitive and easily hurt. They take their emotions inward, and it results in plucking. Other parrots seem less aggressive. That's just my opinion.

Dutch definitely has his opinions too. He likes to

come out of his cage around 8 and eat his breakfast on his playstand. After that, he will climb down to the lowest level and destroy his current favorite toys: compressed cardboard circles. After that, if he has any energy left, he will rip apart a wood block or two.

Around 4, Dutch wants to go back to his cage for a couple of hours. He may or may not want to come out again around 6 or 7.

Day 68:

I put Dutch in his carrier and took him on his first bike ride today. He muttered most of the way to, around the park and back home. He seemed to like it and slept soundly last night. (I did too, finally.)

One of the ladies at the park realized I had a parrot on the bike and excitedly told her friends, "Look! She has a bird!"

Dutch may or may not bite the stick while stepping up. Sometimes he surprises me and bites the stick repeatedly when leaving his playstand. I think he's saying, "You're late! I wanted to go back to my cage a half hour ago! So take that, you stupid stick!"

For a few days, I've been handling Dutch with a glove on my right hand and he was doing great. I thought about it and decided that, since falconers handle their birds with a glove, I should be okay doing it too. But I should have worn double thick leather gloves instead of my thin leather riding gloves or put a muzzle on Dutch because today he bit me through the glove, and broke the flesh! The only reason I could find that might have caused him to bite was either the glove was on my left hand or he was punishing the "stupid" glove for being late.

I dropped him on the mat by the couch and he ran over and bit my night stand. I picked him up again with the glove on, and said, "Why did you do that, big bird?" Luckily, he didn't bite me again.

Day 69:

Dutch and I had a quiet day. We went for another bike ride and he seemed to enjoy it. After our ride, I put Dutch back in his cage so he could get a drink of water and a bite to eat. He climbed right in and seemed happy.

Soon, it seemed like he wanted to come out again so I put on my glove and he got on the perch by the cage door. I opened the door and said "Wanna come out?" I offered my right (gloved) hand and he bit me! I let him drop to the bottom of the cage and he walked to the back corner and he put his head in the corner.

I sat down on the couch and Dutch climbed up on his favorite perch and started hollering really loud. So I got off the couch and covered his cage. He hollered for a while, then shut up.

Later, I uncovered him and said "Wanna come out?" Dutch came out peacefully, without putting his beak on the glove. I put him on his playstand and he ate a little, then climbed down and destroyed his paper toys. Then he took a nap. I left him there another half hour and then put him in his cage for the night.

I don't think I'll ever understand why Dutch bites.

Day 70:

Dutch and I had a quiet day He called a little, and not loudly, when I went into another room and left him on his playstand, but he stopped calling when he heard me making noises in the other room.

I decided to give Dutch a new toy to destroy. He seemed fascinated by the sound cellophane makes when I unwrap things, so I poked a hole in a piece of cellophane and strung it up with his wood toys. He eye-balled it for a while, then grabbed it and tried to tear it apart for a minute or two. Then he lost interest. He couldn't rip the cellophane apart, and he never touched in again.

Day 71:

We had another nice, quiet day. I have no clue why some days are better than others. I wonder if Dutch knows.

Day 72:

Dutch and I took a bike ride around the park

with Linda. He seemed to enjoy it. Linda and I kept talking to him and he grunted back at us.

I was surprised when, after I put Dutch in his cage and covered him for the night, he called loudly for quite a while. I thought he would be tired after our ride and sleep peacefully, but that wasn't the case. Why?

Day 73:
Today I saw 3 instances of Dutch thinking, putting facts together and drawing conclusions. The first was when I got off the couch to get my phone from the charger on my desk. Dutch had been sleeping on the lowest level of his playstand. He opened his eyes and grunted. When I sat back down on the couch, he closed his eyes and went back to sleep.

The second time, I opened his cage door in the afternoon and said, "Wanna come out?" Dutch was sitting on his highest perch at the back of his cage and he answered my question by turning around on his perch and facing the back of his cage.

The 3rd time was later in the evening. I wanted to let him have one more opportunity to get out of the cage before I would cover him for the night. I opened the cage door and said, "Wanna come out?" Dutch was still on his high perch, and he started to come down to make his way to the door, but his path was blocked by another perch and a new toy, so he turned around and climbed up the side of the cage, across the top (hanging upside down and using his beak as a third leg) and down the side of the cage to the perch by the door. I know these are simple instances of thinking, but it's thinking nonetheless, and observing that makes me happy.

Day 74:

Dutch seemed to be reverting a little today. He bit the stick angrily but stepped up anyway this morning. I put him back on the cage door and made him step up nicely like a "Good bird" When I put him on his playstand, I fully intended to make him step up nicely 2 or 3 more times, but he rushed off and started eating his breakfast right away, so I let it go.

Later on, when I went into another room, he started to grunt, then call, but he stopped after a minute and seemed to be listening. When I said "What?" he started calling again, so that was my mistake. I'm still learning. Maybe I am an idiot.

We had a nice day after that. Dutch really likes his vegetables but ignores his pellets so I put the pellets in a separate dish. He can eat them or not, I don't care. From the ingredients, the pellets I bought (organic, freeze dried, non-GMO, in other words, expensive) seem to be legume and grass. I would ignore them too. I ordered him some organic, freeze dried, non-GMO fruits. He didn't like them either.

One thing he likes for sure is boiled peanuts. I'm a southern girl and I grew up eating boiled peanuts. Yankees usually don't like them, but Dutch is a southern bird. His species is native to Mexico and South America. At least we have that in common.

Dutch knows what I have for us the minute I come out of the kitchen with the paper plate covered by a napkin. If he's high up on the playstand, he rushes down and gets as close to me as possible to make sure I don't eat them all.

I'm trying to get Dutch to say "Want some" but, so far, I'm the only one saying it. I'm also trying to get him to say: "Wanna come out?" "Hi," "Step up," and "What's up?" Today he threw me a bone and said. "Hi" three times! It made me very happy.

Day 75:

We had a wonderful day! Dutch stepped up only once with aggression, and I made him repeat it peacefully twice after that. He didn't holler once during the many times I tested him by going into other rooms. He even clucked back to me once when I clucked to him. He wouldn't do it again, though, when I clucked twice more. He just looked at me like, "Yeah, you're doing it right."

I'm also trying to teach Dutch to lift a foot when I say "Hi!" So far, I can only get him to lift a foot after I get him to "turn around" but he is fairly consistent about lifting the foot and holding it up after he turns around, and that's when I say a big "Hi!" in my bright, happy voice. He doesn't join in the conversation, though. He just looks at me. Maybe he's thinking, "I made her say hi again. I thinks she's trainable. There might be hope for her."

Day 76:

Today Dutch started to holler when I had been in another room for about 15 minutes. It sounded like the first word I tried to teach him: "Shar-wot!" I listened and he said it a few more times. Definitely "Shar-wot!" Unfortunately, I was busy and couldn't go to him, so I said "What?" He just stopped and listened, then started up again. After calling a few more times, and me responding, he switched to "Ah, ah, ah," his original call. I don't know if that was an opportunity lost or progress.

Day 77:

After a quiet morning, Dutch was hormonal again this afternoon, crouching on his perch, quivering and muttering, "Ah, ah" repeatedly. Only this time, he focused on something out the patio doors, instead of on me.

Later, I learned that a blue and gold macaw was loose in the neighborhood. Two of my neighbors saw it in the tree by my patio. I, however, did not see it, but I guess Dutch did.

Day 78:

It has been a week since Dutch chewed up the vet wrap on his perches. I don't know if he lost interest or something has changed. He has also quit shredding his cardboard circles, his other favorite toy. I don't know what has changed. His macaw friend has been captured and I think he must be sad.

Day 79:

Dutch was quiet all day, even when I was in other rooms for extended periods of time. Later in the day, I looked at the photos I took of him at the rescue and compared them to recent photos. I could see a big difference in his feathers. They look brighter.

Dutch spends a lot of time grooming himself. He sends feather dust floating through the air and it lands on everything, including me. He sheds a lot of short downy feathers and a few longer feathers too.

I'm excited to see his flight feathers grow out. Currently, he has all of them clipped for some reason. Usually, only 4 are clipped. I really don't think he will fly when he grows new ones. He has probably spent his whole life not flying and I don't think he will have the muscle strength necessary for flight when they grow out.

He has also gained weight. Maybe too much, but I'm not worried about that. I figure he needs the extra weight to molt and grow new feathers.

Day 80:

Dutch was good earlier in the day, even when I was in the kitchen for an extended period of time. But, when I went onto the balcony to fill the bird feeders late in the afternoon, he started yelling and wouldn't stop, even after I caged and covered him. He finally shut up, but didn't want to come out of his cage after that, and was quiet for the rest of the night. I have no idea what he was yelling about.

Day 81:

It was a quiet day. Dutch was briefly hormonal this morning. Other than that, he was quiet and seemed happy.

Day 82:

I ran errands this morning, so Dutch spent a few hours caged and covered. I could tell he slept most of the time because of the large poop pile under the perch he likes to sleep on.

The afternoon was quiet.

Day 83:

Dutch was hormonal again. He got mad at me when I interrupted his "dance" for a short training session. I'm as stubborn as he is, so I insisted that he do what I wanted (turn around and say hi by lifting and holding up a foot) before I let him get back to his ritual.

After 3 hours during which Dutch stopped his "dance" only to eat, I decided to put him back in his cage and cover him. I left him there for a couple of hours, and when he came out, he seemed to have forgotten all about his hormones. Why?

Day 84:

I'm convinced that the reason Dutch bites the step up stick (or my arm or my hand or whatever is offered) is that he's afraid of falling. He uses his beak like a third leg when climbing, so it makes sense that he would use it to step up too. Or maybe it's just a habit developed after falling a few times.

Day 85:

Today, after weeks of procrastination, I had to scrub my floors. I put Dutch in his cage, thinking he would eat and sleep since he knew where I was, but he started yelling and wouldn't stop, even though I talked to him. So I covered him. He just yelled louder. For an hour. When I finished working and uncovered him, he stopped yelling. Unless he can see me or hear me doing familiar things, he isn't happy? I really don't know.

Day 86:

Dutch left me a wing feather in his food dish. It

is beautiful with colors flowing from green to blue to black. That means (I hope) that he is molting and growing new flight feathers. I want him to have all his flight feathers in case he falls. Then he will be able to glide to the floor. But all his flight feathers had been cut when I got him and it will take a year to grow them back. I don't think he will ever fly. I think he has been clipped for over 20 years and his flight muscles never developed. An that's probably why he bites the stick to step up. He must have a huge fear of falling. Just a guess.

Day 87:

The day started out peacefully. Dutch didn't yell when I disappeared into the bedroom for more than an hour. I could hear him grunting "baby grunts" now and then, but they didn't escalate into yelling.

Later, before I could prevent it, Dutch jumped onto my hand. I stiffened, but the feared bite didn't come. He was soft in his grip with his feet so I cautiously put him back on his playstand and told him he was a "Good bird!" He seemed to want to get on my hand again, but I wasn't interested in pushing my luck!

Later in the day, Dutch was grooming himself, preening his feathers and, after sitting there, watching him with my cell phone camera, I was able to get good photos of his wings spread out and I could also see that he was growing one new flight feather. I'm anxious to see him grow all his flight feathers out, even if it means he might be able to dive-bomb and bite me.

Actually, I think the biting will be less when he has all his flight feathers. And I think people who clip their birds flight feathers are equivalent to those who hobble horses Sometimes it's necessary, but sometimes it's just cruel. Anyone who denies an animal it's basic and only method of escape is cruel, in my opinion.

Day 88:

Today was a good day. Dutch was quiet. Nothing seemed to bother him and guess what? He loves barbecue potato chips as much as I do!

Day 89:

Today I put a storage box on the bottom shelf of Dutch's playstand. The box holds all the things he loves to tear up: his vet wrap, paper toys and colored wood blocks. The playstand has an inverted seed catcher skirt at the bottom of his area, above the storage shelf, so it's almost impossible for him to see what's below it. But Dutch is clever. He crawled down his favorite perch and balanced on the thin edge of the skirt to take a look at the box stored down there. He kept turning his head and looking at it, first with his left eye, then his right eye. Finally, he was satisfied and climbed back onto his perch on the playstand. I was impressed!

Day 90:

Today Dutch threw me another bone. I had a cup of coffee, and every time I took a sip and stared at him, he would make a gurgling noise. I was delighted! It's embarrassing how small gestures from that aggressive green chicken wraps around my heart and makes me coo "Good bird!"

MY LAST DAYS WITH DUTCH

Day 91:

Today Dutch was aggressive and loud. I had to cage and cover him while I opened my door (he could see me, so why was he loud?) and drug in 3 boxes from Amazon. I opened the boxes and put the smallest one in the bottom of his cage so he could tear it up and get his aggression out.

Even after tearing the box up, he hollered. It sounded like "Ha, ha, ha" over and over. No wonder my downstairs neighbor thought it was me 3 months ago, screaming for help!

Day 92:

Dutch was so angry today that he spent most of the day in his cage, both covered and uncovered. After being on his playstand for an hour, I put him back in his cage. Later, he showed no desire to step up on the stick and come out of the cage. He would just look at it or attack it.

Finally, I had to get him out of his cage to clean it, and I had to insist that he step up.

After cleaning the cage, I put another small box in the bottom of his cage. I wondered if he wanted to make a nest, but he just spent a couple of hours attacking it and chewing it up.

Day 93:

We had a totally quiet, peaceful day! What changed?

Day 94:

It was another quiet and peaceful day. I repeat: What changed?

Day 95:

Another peaceful day. Dutch was quiet when I went into another room, sometimes sleeping on the bottom perch on his playstand the whole time I was absent. That's new...

Day 96:

Have we crossed a threshold? Dutch continues to be quiet when I'm in another room. Maybe he's feeling secure now. I hope so. Maybe he will start talking soon. That would be great!

I had steak tonight and Dutch got a piece too. So far, he likes chicken, ham, beef, nuts, seeds and vegetables. He doesn't care for fruit. I guess he's on a keto diet?

Day 97:

We had another quiet day.

After 2 months of shedding and filling the air with dust, Dutch is still molting. Today he left me a short green feather (probably a guard feather from a wing) and another long wing feather. That's good. I hope it means he will grow out all his flight feathers.

Dutch spends most of the day sitting on the playstand skirt, pooping over the edge. Thankfully, I had the foresight to buy a rubber mat to lay over the carpet under his playstand. I got one for his cage, too, to catch all the dust and food he flings out of the cage. As they say, owning a parrot is like owning a perpetual two year old.

Day 98:

Every time I asked Dutch to step up on the stick today, he bit it, so he had to repeat it until he stepped up without biting. Then I made a big fuss and told him he's a "Good bird!" in the loud, silly voice he loves. I'm getting paranoid. Is he biting the stick just to go through that routine and hear "Good bird?" Is this just another way of training me?

Day 99:

We had a wonderful, quiet day today until 7 in the evening when Dutch suddenly reached out and bit my index finger as I was giving him a nut. I put him in his cage and covered him.

What happened?

Tomorrow I'm pricing pit bulls and tarantulas.

DUTCH GETS A NEW HOME:

Day 100:

After a restless night, and coughing and sneezing until I got a headache, I made a decision. I had to find a new home for Dutch. I was definitely allergic to him and buying a 4th air cleaner wouldn't fix the problem.

I didn't want to send Dutch back to the rescue where they would clip his flight feathers and adopt him out to another unsuspecting and hopeful home. So I called my friend Linda and asked her if she knew of anyone silly enough to give Dutch a new home. I told her I wasn't in a hurry, but she called me back the same day and said her niece, Michelle, wanted to meet Dutch.

Michelle had an African Grey parrot. That's a good start, I thought, but worlds away from a character like my bird.

So she came to meet Dutch.

Dutch was on his best behavior. We sat down and talked right in front of him for a while. I had put him on the playstand before she arrived just in case, well, you know. I told her Dutch might bite for un-known reasons, but she was welcome to try to hold him, so Michelle asked him to step up. Dutch gently walked onto her hand and looked at me like, "See? That's how you do it."

She fell in love with him.

I cautioned her to be careful and not let him get near her shoulder or face and I'm sure Dutch was thinking, "What's the problem?"

Michelle said she would take him, so we arranged for her to pick him up with all his belongings the next day. Dutch has a lot of stuff, but her husband has a truck.

DAY 101:

Her husband, Jake, was probably surprised at how much stuff Dutch owned, had to re-arrange his stuff in the truck bed to accommodate Dutch's stuff.

Fortunately, I had timed everything just right, putting Dutch in the carrier (using the step-up stick, of course) right before they pulled into the apartment building parking lot.

Jake had agreed to take Dutch right away, when Linda made the call, so I wasn't worried about having to unbox all his stuff when an unsuspecting husband discovered what his wife had done.

DAY 102:

Jake fell in love with Dutch! And it seems the feeling was mutual I received a text update and a photo of him holding Dutch that very evening.

But the African Grey was not in love. His name is Buddy. Right away, he asked Dutch, "Are you a good bird?"

Dutch probably just looked at him and thought, "Eat your heart out, grey bird. I'm here and I'll be taking over."

That evening, when Michelle and Jake left the livingroom, where both birds have their cages and playstands, to eat dinner in the diningroom, Dutch began to yell. "Help! Help! Help!"

Buddy yelled back, "Shut up!"

The drama had begun...

also by Charlotte Godfrey:

THE HORSE CONNECTION part 1

horses, love and loss

THE HORSE CONNECTION part 2

horses, friendship and revenge

THE HORSE CONNECTION part 3

growing pains

Loving Mother

and leaving her at any cost

BOARDING STABLE RANTS

why barn owners are crazy!

Learn to Ride!

Introducing horse care and riding

ROADAPPLES...

Droppings from a lifetime with horses...

FABULOUS FORWARDS

14 years of e-mail fun

AGING FORWARDS

From Fabulous Forwards

THE HORSE CONNECTION part 1

horses, love and loss

I went to work the next day after school, as usual, grabbed my wheelbarrow and pitchfork and started on the first stall. I was working on the second one when the idiots appeared in the doorway of the stall. I was trapped.

"Hey, thanks for getting the hay for us yesterday," Ray said. "And it was really nice of you to give us the rest of the afternoon off."

I just looked at him while the anger was building up inside me.

"Yeah, Max was a little upset with you, though," Ray said with a smirk on his face. "He thought you were getting a little uppity, taking over like that, and acting like you was the boss. And you owe us," he added, "or else we will tell Max you dumped us just to be a bitch when we left the truck to go pee."

Then Ray turned to Joe. "Wanna go first?"

Joe smiled and shook his head. "Go ahead, bro. You go first."

Ray stepped into the stall. Then he spread his legs and unbuckled his belt.

I didn't ask him what he was doing. I just hit him hard on his stupid head with the business end of my pitchfork. I was really glad it was the old-fashioned metal kind. But Ray wasn't. He crumbled like an empty burlap sack.

Joe was a little slow to react. He just stood there with his mouth open, watching Ray fall. That gave me enough time to grab the wheelbarrow and slam it into his knees. He fell as gracelessly as his bro. Just for fun, I emptied the contents of the wheelbarrow on his face.

I didn't stick around after that. I grabbed my bicycle and went home. It was Friday, so I told my mother we ran out of work early and quit for the day.

I didn't work at the Silver Spur on the weekends. The boys were going to get a couple of days to think about things. I just hoped they were smart enough to figure out that I won't be messed with when I went back to work on Monday.

But Max called my mother and said I was fired.

By then, I guess she had enough of me getting fired, because that's when she decided to get rid of me.

THE HORSE CONNECTION part 2
horses, friendship and revenge

Irene's husband arrived at dinnertime. Everyone, even Cyra, gathered at The Meadows Restaurant to have dinner together. Tomorrow afternoon, the show would be over, and everyone would be packing up to leave. Dinner would consist of left-overs from the concession stand on the show grounds or snacks bought at stops during the drive home. But tonight, we would feast and celebrate the events of the day.

The restaurant was packed, so we gathered at the bar for drinks, and stood in a circle and talked as we waited for our table. A few minutes after our drinks were served, Irene's husband walked into the bar area. He was spotted first by the twins. "Joey!" they cried in unison.

"Hey-hey!" Joey answered, patting them both on the back and squeezing them together in a hug. "What's zup?" Joey wasn't overweight, but he was big, although shorter than Al, who I suddenly missed. Like Al usually did, he wore a dark suit. But Joey's tie, not like Al's typical tie, was wide, bright and multi-colored. It seemed to add a cheery note to the already festive atmosphere.

"Irene's up!" Layne answered. "She has her first score for her Gold Medal! Only three more to go!"

"Hey, hey, hey, Layne!" Joey gave Layne a hug and looked for his wife in the crowd. Finding her, he pushed through and grabbed her,

"Irene! Babe! You did good!" He hugged and kissed her loudly, not noticing that she looked uncomfortable.

Then he spotted Bonnie. "Bonnie! How are you, my love?" Bonnie got a hug too.

Joey looked around. "Where's our table? Why aren't we seated? Didn't you call in a reservation?" His questions weren't directed at anyone in particular, so no one answered, and Joey didn't wait for an answer. "Wait here. I'll be back," he said to no one in particular.

"That's my Joey," Irene said with a little smile as she watched him disappear into the crowd.

"Yeah, he'll get us a table and fast!" Layne said, laughing.

I watched as Joey approached the hostess at the desk. He asked her a question, and she shook her head. Then he asked her another question. She looked at him. He shifted his weight and put a hand in his pocket. The hostess consulted her table chart and looked up. She said something to Joey, and he smiled, put his hand on her shoulder and gestured toward the dining room with his other hand. The hostess picked up a stack of menus and Joey took them from her, putting something in her hand as he took them.

Then Joey walked back to his wife. "Okay! We can eat! Follow the young lady!" Joey waved us toward the smiling hostess.

We were given a large round table at the back of the restaurant. Without a doubt it was the best table in the restaurant and, also without a doubt, it was because Joey made it happen.

THE HORSE CONNECTION part 3

growing pains

I waited as the guard unlocked the gates. She pushed them open for me, and I walked through to freedom.

"Thanks," I said.

"Don't come back," she joked.

"Not a chance."

I had my suitcase, some money and my life back. Five years gone. A 27-year-old was. My dreams hadn't died, and neither had my anger. But now, thanks to anger management classes, I had the skill to hide it, control it be patient and plan my revenge.

No one met me at the gate. I was alone. My husband divorced me as soon as I was incarcerated. I had only one visitor while I was waiting in the county jail for my trial. Marsha came once and brought me some money. She never came back, but she sent me a few dollars each month through the prison's system of handling an inmate's cash. And I hadn't heard from anyone at Centerline or from the club during the past five years. It was their loss. I wouldn't forget it, either.

The one thing I really missed was horses. I spent my entire life with horses since I was eight years old. I missed my horse Marlboro the most, and I intended to see him soon. That is, I hoped to see him. I hoped Bonnie had kept him at the farm for me, and I hoped she had taken care of his tendon injury, too. At any rate, I intended to find out as soon as possible.

Marlboro was five years older now and should have healed. I hoped he was still being ridden. He was training at Grand Prix when he was injured during turnout in a pasture. Alone. No one seemed to know how he got hurt. That was suspicious, and I still thought it might have been caused by one of the many barn helpers I fired when I worked at Centerline. Barn help? More like barn harm, I thought. Anyway, he should have healed by now.

I shifted my suitcase to my left hand and took a deep breath of free air. It smelled good. But not fresh. I could detect diesel fumes and asphalt in it, but it smelled good, anyway. Prison air smelled like sweat and urine. When we got outside for 2 hours a day, the air smelled like sweat and cigarette smoke. I didn't smoke and I used deodorant. Yes, diesel and asphalt definitely smelled better.

No one was meeting me, and I didn't have a ride. I walked away from the Women's Huron Valley Correctional Facility and onto Bemis Road. I headed east on Bemis because I knew it would cross 23 and then connect with I-94. After I got on 23, I walked backwards and stuck out my thumb when I saw a tractor trailer approaching. I was still skinny and attractive. I got a ride.

The trucker who picked me up was middle-aged, had a day-old beard and smelled sweaty. "Where are you headed?" he asked when I got in.

"Port Huron."

"Well, you're in luck. I'm headed to Canada through Port Huron." The trucker put his turn signal on and eased back into traffic.

"Great." I looked in the back of his cab. It had a bedroll in it. "You sleep back there?"

"Sometimes. Sometimes I use it for other things," he grinned, but got no response from me, so he said,"Why are you hitching? What's your story?"

"I just got out of prison."

The trucker's eyebrows shot up. I could see that I had earned a little respect. "What were you in for?"

"Murder. I killed a woman."

The trucker looked at me. "How? Did you shoot her?"

"No, I beat her to death."

"Wow," he laughed nervously. "You must have been really mad."

"I still am."

Loving Mother

and leaving her at any cost

"Your mother has had an accident and you need to come home."

Home. There was that word again. My shoulders dropped. Would I ever be free of this woman? Every time I thought I had gotten free, I found myself returning home again. I let out a deep sigh. I had been stupid to think that I could be free.

"Is she gonna die?" I asked.

"No, but she needs 24 hour care."

It suddenly occurred to me that I would have to be the caregiver. My breathing stopped. I felt my stomach knot up. Was there any escape from this woman? Would my life always be tied to hers? 24 hour care? I couldn't breathe.

BOARDING STABLE RANTS

why barn owners are crazy!

FORWARD

This book was written after 45 years in the business of boarding horses. It was born out of hard work, joys and tears, fights and victories, rescues, puzzelments and bitch sessions.

I hope it will make you smile or laugh. If it makes you angry, maybe I've hit a nerve or fleshed out a truth.

The truth is that it's difficult to be a boarder who has to trust someone else to care for their most precious animal and it's difficult to be a boarding stable owner who has to balance all the aspects of running a business with being an unpaid psychologist.

And now that I've managed to ruffle the feathers of both boarders and boarding stable owners, let's see if I can do some more damage in the following pages...

DEDICATION

This book is dedicated to the memory of my husband, Joel, who firmly believed that horses were livestock until the day we divorced.

NOTE

In this book, I refer to the boarding stable owner and the boarder as "you". I might not be referring directly to you as the subject of my rant but, I could be if the boot fits!

I'm gonna step on a few toes. I've been in this business too long to be nice about the issues in this book. I've wrangled with them almost every day of my life for the last 45 years and it's time to vent, so put on your shit-kickin' boots and join me!

RoadApples...
TABLE OF CONTENTS

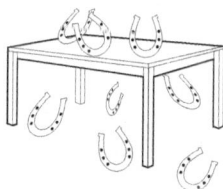

Learn to Ride!
Introducing horse care and riding

TO THE NEW HORSEMAN:

Learn to Ride! is a guide, written for young horsemen, but it has been proven to be useful and fun for new horsemen of any age. I suggest that any new horseman of any age find an instructor to act as a mentor when using this guide.

Please write in this book:
There is a place for your name and places to make notes. There are questions throughout the book about each chapter. You can answer the questions - either with your instructor or at home by yourself. Some questions are about things not discussed in this book. I asked them to make you THINK and to discuss them with your instructor or find the answers online. It's fun to not know something and learn the answer!

With the help of this book, searching online or asking your instructor, you will learn to halter, groom, show a horse in-hand, help tack up your horse and ride a beginner dressage test.

Welcome to the wonderful world of horses!

Charlotte Godfrey

FABULOUS FORWARDS
14 years of forwarding fun!

INTRODUCTION

It was the year 2000 and I didn't know how to turn on a computer. That was fine with my husband. He wanted me at home, taking care of him and pretty much ignorant of the outside world, except for TV news, which was unavoidable since he watched it every night. But I was curious and I requested a computer for Christmas. My husband brought home an old desktop from his workplace with Windows 94 on it. No internet.

I asked my girlfriend, Sandi, to give me a lesson on computers, "Teach me how a computer works," I said. She giggled and rubbed her hands together. "Okay! Welcome to the modern world! This is how you turn it on. Now what do you want to do?"

"I don't know." I said, "Just teach me a little about them." So, she proceeded to tell me that computers are based on files and folders, and my eyes glazed over. First typing, then files and folders? Ugh. I hated typing in high school and barely passed the class. Files and folders? It sounded boring.

But she continued to teach me. Computers, she said, can be highly organized tools. I really like organization. So I learned about files and folders and I became a fairly good typist.

By January, I was longing to be on the internet and find out what the big deal was, so I called a dial-up company and got online. Then the emails started coming in from all my computer savy friends! What a hoot! The fun was unbelievable! So I copied the best forwards, pasted them into files and put them in folders... for fourteen years!

Now it appears that texting is replacing emailing friends and the once enjoyable experience of email has become a slush pile of advertisement and con artist scams. I came to realize that I had enjoyed an "era" which has pretty much passed.

This book is an effort to preserve, in my own way, the fun that emailing once gave us. I urge you to copy some of these forwards and send them to your friends. Have fun!

AGING FORWARDS
14 years of forwarding fun!

LIFE BEGINS AT FIFTY

Maybe it's true that life begins at fifty...
But thats when everything else starts to wear out,
fall out, or spread out.

About the Author:

Charlotte Godfrey's first horse was her Grandpop's mule, Maggie, who she jumped bareback - until Pop found her on the ground after jumping an obstacle under Granny's wire clothes line. When he discovered that she wasn't decapitated, he forbade her to jump and bought her a horse who tried to kill her in other ways. That horse, who knew several ways of getting rid of children, taught her about self-preservation and confirmed in her a life-long love of horses and dressage.

photograph by
Michael Sexton

Her next horse, after a child, college, marriage, divorce and re-marriage (in that order, but repeat a few steps...) was a Quarter Horse named Oliver, who was obtained by blackmailing her husband and threatening the owner. After Charlotte added 2 more horses to the board bill, her husband decided that it would be cheaper and more tax-advantageous to buy property and build their own boarding stable! He built a barn, purchased a horse trailer, dug a pond, constructed an outdoor arena, an indoor arena, more stalls...and so on...

Running a boarding stable proved to be such a delightful way to lose money that, after her divorce, Charlotte and 2 unfortunate partners: Mike and her mother, Milly, joined up to buy an even bigger boarding stable.

Charlotte is pictured above with her horse, Gotsno, or "Mr. Wonderful," as he prefers to be known...

If you enjoyed this book, please leave a review.

www.ingramcontent.com/pod-product-compliance
Lightning Source LLC
Chambersburg PA
CBHW020554030426
42337CB00013B/1091